Ross McFarlane writes soft and k
weak Glaswegian accent far too ·
He wants to write with the perfec
stir up heady excitement in a cro
and draw you slowly into a Craig Finn-esk world of his own
creation.

Self-styled "Glasgow's No. 1 Support Act", Ross has opened
for touring poets and musicians alike including; Sabrina
Benaim, Shane Koyczan, Rudy Fransisco, Rae Spoon, Petrol
Girls, Throw Me Off The Bridge, and Jesus and his Judgmental
Father. Catch him on the MegaBuses searching for touring
musicians to accost with poetry.

Check out more stories by Ross through In The Works
spoken word theatre company, where he has written for and
performed in productions including *A Matter of Time* and *The
900 Club*, as well as touring the UK and Ireland with millennial
drama *Make/Shift*. He is a writer and producer on queer horror
audio drama *Folxlore*, which has won the Audio Verse Award
for Best New Storytelling Production, and featured in The
Atlantic's 50 Best Podcasts of 2020.

One day, he will build his commune. You will all be invited.

Life Goals of Millennials:

or The Commune Manifesto

Ross McFarlane

Burning Eye

BurningEyeBooks
Never Knowingly
Mainstream

This first edition published by Burning Eye Books 2022

www.burningeye.co.uk

@burningeyebooks

Burning Eye Books
15 West Hill, Portishead, BS20 6LG

ISBN 978-1-913958-21-3

For Bibi. For Neil. For Leisha.
For Ellen. For Syd. For Shannon.
For the punks and poets, friends close and far.
I hope to see you home one day, wherever that is.

CONTENTS

Life Goals of Millennials:
or The Commune Manifesto   9

Never making the first move, and other
unbreakable habits   12

Sunday Morning, 2015   15

Small Requests from
Commuter Town Kids   16

Hi (Bi Boy)   17

A Crowded Table, 2017   19

St Christopher of the Club Scene   20

Dinner and Doses   22

No Sleep Till We Feel Better   23

A Palate Cleanser   25

I used to be an antitheist,
then I made some gods   26

Hair Dye, 2019   28

RSVP to the Queer Prom   29

Time Travel Party   29

2040   30

LIFE GOALS OF MILLENNIALS: OR THE COMMUNE MANIFESTO

Are you saving up for a deposit?
You know you're wasting money when you rent?
Why won't you own a home by twenty-four?

If you'd stayed with your parents, waited, saved,
not been born thirty years too late
then you'd have your own place already!

But hey,
no point assigning blame.
They just capitalised on capitalism.
You would have done the same.

But we're the kids of contradictions.

Brought up with the belief we could do anything,
growing up to see that construct crumbling,
yet we still want what our parents got.
A place of our own; that can't be a lot?

Well, I've been thinking –
since I moved back and walking home became the walk to
    isolation.

I've been thinking –
is a place for me and mine what I want from a living situation?

I've been thinking –
how many contradictions can fit inside one person?

I've been asking –
is that really all I'm missing?

I miss coming home to someone I know will keep me afloat,
'cause we're both rowing from the same boat

I just want a ten-bed in the West End with my best friends.

See, my home is from that hippy scene.
It's all finger-clicks and tambourines.

In my home,
we brew alcohol from aniseed,
watch the audience like Amelie
and read the papers like they're fantasies.

In my home,
Shannon's got a bag of weed in a fake book
on the mantelpiece.

The stereo is blasting *Grease*
while Alex sings in harmonies
to Sandra Dee.

In my home,
Lauren's advocating anarchy,
Leisha's acting cavalier,
Nik's coming back from Calgary.

In my home,
apathy is blasphemy.

We catch the feels so hard it seems
as though our hearts could bleed.
We build our blankets into canopies.

In my home,
we seek comfort from catastrophes
and stand in solidarity.

Every past defeat's a masterpiece.
We're crafting dreams.
You can't believe the carpentry.

In my home,
we've created our own sanctuary,
sewn all of our tattered seams
into one magnificent tapestry.

In my home,
we've taken all our tapped-out beats
and turned them to a rhapsody.

In my home,
my friends become a part of me.

In our home,
not one of us will act as judge.

In our home,
we are nothing but this fucking love.

In all honesty –
I just want to feel at home in a place where I don't feel alone.

So fuck a whole ocean, I'll take the stone's throw.

Fuck the doom and the gloom,
even for a stylish two-bedroom.
I'm crawling out of this costume.
I'll catch you all at the commune.

NEVER MAKING THE FIRST MOVE, AND OTHER UNBREAKABLE HABITS

I got this advice from a YouTube video – I guess that you can have it. It takes three months, 100 days, of repetition for you to form a habit, and three months ago this is how mine started:

Day 1
It's the last day of my exam stress, and I'm blessed to be sitting outside on a manky bench in the presence of my best friends and a pint of Tennent's.

(The union do it for a quid if you bring in your last test paper.)

We deserve the chance to relax and savour the climax of four years of hard labour; of late-night library times, one hundred thousand words typed, and the idea that the letters we're presented must define our whole lives...

Then he walks in, and changes mine. Not in that second, as you're led to expect, but in retrospect I can tell.

We tip some back; start living lavish. Starved of freedom, we are lifting famine. Spark some interest and some party anthems. Mark our hours by the cigs we're passing. After some time, me and him start chatting

Talking close, I think I have it till he checks his phone and has to dash quick, but all it took was that little magic that his smile and laughter captured. That was me; that's the part when I began to start my habit.

Day 2
Not *just* a friend request...

But an immediate message upon acceptance, and I confess I'm a little less than hesitant or tentative in my response

Day 10
We've been chatting on and off; he tells me he's got a blog.
I check it out – offer help with Photoshop or, if he wants, I do
headshots.

Day 24
I got him listening to The Boss. Online still, got no time off. It
would be nice to get together, talk, put on a record. For now
our messages get longer and I waste time each day wondering
what his face looks like in the amber rays of a sunrise through
my blinds.

Day 68
He's been away for thirty days. I would say I miss him, but that
would be a little much; it's only been a couple months.

Honestly, I don't know if he feels the same; I'm still guessing
at this stage. But next week we'll meet up, see each other, see
what happens. He's said he's not much of a flirt, but so far…

I think he's managed.

Day 79
We had a lovely time – I guess? We listened to his singles, we
sat out of my window smoking cigarettes and singing all the
words we could remember.

And then he left.

I wonder if I misread it? Maybe we're better off as friends, and
hey, I get it. I do.

I just want another hit of feeling wanted like I did when I
thought that that boy wanted me like ice cream wants a kid,
like roses wanted sniffed, like Eve wanted a rib to live, like I
had wanted him.

But I would be remiss to disguise this unrequitedness or to

make the burden his. Before I'm resigned to being chased – I ought to ask him on a date.

Day 80
He says that 'that sounds nice'.

Day 81
We set a time.

Day 95
I'm quite excited.

Day 98
Hyperventilate.

Day 99
It's almost time.

Day 100
He's all blinking lips and smiling eyes, and I drink him in but I'm kinda shy; he twists his fingers and I think I'll try... I mean, that look he shoots me might imply.

I kiss him quick. He smiles. I sigh. I touch his hips and we say *good night.*

As we glance back, as a warmth grows inside, as we make tracks back to our flats after a night of anxious relaxing and salacious surprise – I wonder how I would have felt three months ago if I'd seen myself.

His smile like Springsteen when our lips meet with a click of teeth, and I feel sixteen in that river scene. The mystery of how this would feel becomes clear to me. There's a chill between my skinny jeans and my trembling knees. I remember the adage – breaking a habit ain't the same as taking the last hit.

SUNDAY MORNING, 2015

Blurry eye open,
sleep in its corners.

Chapped lips
        pressed gently
                against a neck,
remnants of red wine and cigarettes.

Arms entangled,
            legs bent.

They show no intent of leaving this bed.

Jeans and T-shirts like seabed creatures
huddled in bundles going nowhere – slowly.

It's just that kind of Sunday.

Condensation on the window
shows a faded *I love you*
in drunken, but loving,
calligraphy.

SMALL REQUESTS FROM
COMMUTER TOWN KIDS

Could I have thoughts of something softer?
A greasy kiss outside the chippy.
No passing shouts to make us run,
no passing cars to tell our mums.

Something public, something private,
somewhere we didn't have to hide it.
I could have left your bedroom in the shirt you just had on.

Could you be someone that I'm proud of?
Someone I would have shown off.
Not what we had and how we wore it,
but every day like your cowlick.
Something I'd tell everyone.

Could this memory stay with me now all the hurt has gone?
The best of first romances,
the I'm-so-glad-we-had-this,
not this thing-that-never-was.

Can I think back without regret?
Can I not get sad for once?
Not consider what could have –
not wonder if you had –
or what I should have done.

What if I'd lived somewhere bigger?
What if I'd been somewhat braver?
What if you had been the finger
flicking on the lighter's flint?
What if we had been the friction?

Can I have thoughts of something softer?
The queer teenage romance I never got.
Imagine back, and just enjoy the thought.

HI (BI BOY)

Meet a girl, fall in love

Meet a boy
Meet a straight boy
Meet a nervous boy
Meet a boy who makes you nervous

Meet a girl, fall in love

Meet a boy
Meet a *straight* boy
Meet a friend
Meet a boy who needs a friend

Meet a girl, fall in love

Meet a person
Meet a person at the wrong time
Meet a person, but you're in love
Meet a person, not in love

Meet a girl, fall in love

Meet another boy
Meet the boy and spend a night enraptured
Meet the boy a second time, excited
Meet the boy who met the girl, fell in love

Meet boys who like you 'cause you don't look like you like
boys

Meet boys who like you till they find out you like girls

Meet no one for a while

Meet someone at the back of every bar, at the end of every
   gig, in the breath after a confession, who asks you about
   the boys you've met and loved

I promise you
I met a boy I could have loved
I met a boy I could have loved
I met a boy I could have loved

A CROWDED TABLE, 2017

Finger and thumb
pick up a morsel of sponge
from a licked-clean dinner plate.

A hearty spread
from Pacific islands to Italian tomato bases
scattered where hands could pass them.

An Ikea feast,
with the fanciest glasses
that get sold in Tesco.

We spend our wired brown envelopes
on salt-crusted bread,
fresh spices and herbs.

ST CHRISTOPHER OF THE CLUB SCENE

I met St Chris in a painted mist, bright lights and smoke machines. Eyes the size of rosaries. He spoke to me:

> 'I like to bask in the present,' said ol' St Chris,
> 'and I got bags full of presents like St Nick.'

We escaped posthaste to a warehouse rave. He said, 'There's this girl there, and you've gotta meet her. The kids in the crowd call her the Great Teacher. I know the guy on the door – we call him St Peter.'

> St. Christopher of the club scene,
> his pockets laced with powder and ash.
> St Christopher of the club scene,
> he's chasing his spirits with romance.

How we made it back to this flat is a mystery. So is how it got this busy. Mirrors littering counters, all white blotches and misty. Keeping tabs on my person in case things start looking shifty.

St Chris is in the corner, looks like he's giving a striptease. His pasty white flesh is a mess with red scratches from his neck down his chest, kinda looks like a vest; he wears them like a crest.

And then there's the rest. Running line after line like it's opening night till they give up the fight and Chris's disciples – they fall like flies in the haze; they're weary, well travelled, they've been up for days

> St Chris and I kept up with a devilish trade.
> *We won't sleep till sun's up or he'll take us away...*

Now, Chris needed cigs when the shops opened up. So we walked to the shop on the corner, through the park, to the pub. We sipped pints in the bright light of our prodigal sun, our throats finally quenched as we coated our lungs. And Chris said:

> 'Ain't this been fun, man, ain't this been fun?
> Do you remember when we were fresh cut?
> D'you remember when our stories were young?
> I'm flying off to a different planet.
> I heard Glasgow's kicking its habit.
> Figured I ought to scrap it.'

When only the dregs were left, I decided to head. Chris rolled another instead.

And I think of St Chris when I'm back in the lights, and how many of his nights don't end up so nice. How many are fuzzy and ugly and druggy. How long he'll hold steady, till it all gets too messy.

> St Christopher of the club scene,
> how many nights have you sat by the phone?
> St Christopher of the club scene,
> how many times have you gone out alone?
> How many nights are you on it, on your own?

DINNER AND DOSES

Why can't it be like this forever?
Why can't we be like this forever?

One more pill and no livers overload. I might quiver from the dose, stick on 'Rivers and Roads' and reminisce.

Tell me. *We can't stay like this because the way we live ain't dangerous, but to take more is. Every day we miss for this fateful bliss is another one drowned in the comedown and, Ross, you gotta come down sometimes.*

And honestly, I know you're probably right in reality.
But what's wrong with just one more night of that ecstasy?

*

Why can't it be like this forever?
Why can't we be like this forever?

1am dinners, shivering from cold, rivers on winter weather roads and all you do is say no.

Times change and, at my age, I need to savour the light days, treasure the memories I've made and remember that the level ain't mileage. It's time spent, tightened to the tether of another person's life, then it's how hard you held them and the blind faith they'll stay. You hope and pray they'll stay.

*

I struggle with the stopping part. Every day's harsh inelegance occasionally gets to me. Sometimes all I need is pillow talk, and pills, and a little bit of love from somebody that I trust. Someone who can let me know when I've had enough. It's time to get back on that real stuff.

NO SLEEP TILL WE FEEL BETTER

We talked about what would be found with us. Or whether we'd ever be found at all. I promised I'd come looking if I hadn't seen you in a while, but that's a little more difficult now.

> We had nights of kitchen couches, coffee
> and the comfort of slipping into infinity.
> Cognitive science and newfangled philosophy.

On the first day we couldn't let go of each other's company, we walked the length of Glasgow. A not-quite-drunk pub crawl, from Partick through Kelvingrove to Mono, then back home. We stayed awake late past the dawn break before parting ways, knowing there would definitely be more of the same.

We talked incessantly and listened intently, first with energy, then with effortless empathy. We'd call each other on our down days, or Fridays, or no-sleep-till-sun spring days, and you'd politely smile as I referred to our cases as terminal.

> We had nights of kitchen couches, coffee
> and the comfort of slipping into infinity.
> Cognitive science and newfangled philosophy.

I've never wanted to hug someone so much in my life, but you only ever hugged me twice. The first time, you left mine after a hard night to go hide your medication because you wanted to stay alive. The second time, you boarded a flight.

We had nights of you crashed out on my couch, copious amounts of coffee in the sightlines of eternity. Caught staring at the crosshairs of infinity. Praying that staying there with our eyes open would keep us from the moment we had to deal with the onus of a new day. Still searching for the solution to Camus' first question of philosophy:

> *Why should you stay here with me?*

I've said it a lot that it's always an option to get gone. But you're across the globe now. No longer a stone's throw, but a whole ocean away. I can't help but contemplate the day where you don't reply to me and I can't tell if it's the time zone or whether you're no longer awake.

Just so you know, if it ever gets too much for you over there, I've got your photo on my wall. You've always got a home here.

I've got couches, coffee,
science and philosophy books too,
and I've got all the time in the world for you.

A PALATE CLEANSER

This shirt looks good tucked in.

Your childhood friend still smells like their parents' home.

Wasabi mayonnaise through a blocked nose.

Parched, morning-after-dry mouth
swilled with fizzy Irn-Bru.

Tracing my fingertips
over the candle wax pentagram
in your living room.

Your voice cracked when you sang that line that always
reminds me of you.

A woodsmoke-pollen-cotton cocktail.

The viscous cool of Guinness.

The sweet notes on morning breath you don't mind.

This story is both happy and queer.

You said 'I love you' naturally.
We haven't grown out of it.

The sky is so colourful.
The light behind the branches.
The angles lined up.
From the window, for a second,
you caught a glimpse of the Sunset Tree.

I USED TO BE AN ANTITHEIST, THEN I MADE SOME GODS

after 'Generations' by Rose Butler - The Magpie Poet

Long ago the gods of old
Ruled iron fist and stranglehold
Countries marched under their flag
Cities burned at their demand
Babies born into their hands
But we have stopped believing
And we have forced them to retreat
Now we only speak of Prometheus
And pomegranate seeds

'Cause we're making our own gods these days

And let me tell you all their names:

Glasgow is the god of home
Where it never rains, it pours
Still the stillness in the centre of our storm
Where we return to from the road
A place we rest our weary souls
It's our sunset in the distance
It's a little glimpse of heaven

My friends are the gods of living
When autonomy seems lonely
You can join us in the kitchen
We're mocking up some Scottish broth
With Indonesian peanut sauce
Veggie sushi, Korean kimchi
Mac and cheese and vegan treats
We're serving up a feast
I saved each of you a seat

We still needed two others
The queer lovers
Wholesome and Hopepunk
They mine lives for the gold dust
Shine bright and don't rust
Our final line, our Rosebud
They defy the eyes of grown-ups
Because we know what came before us
And we still respect the old ones
But we remember what they told us

We can be anything

So we chose to be the medicine
To times made of blind hate and pessimism
Nihilism, we ain't messing with it
We have got a better vision

Our gods are stronger than your honour
They will guide us through the horrors
Home is more than brick and mortar
Life is more than bread and water
This world is more than death and monsters
These are what our deities have offered

So we're making our own gods these days
It's to Glasgow, my friends and the Hopepunk that I pray

HAIR DYE, 2019

Matte bleach through sticky gloves.
Dry hair blondes as we talk

and you tell me –
layer swiftly. No skimping. Don't hesitate.
Lap it on. Decisions must come quickly.

Start in the middle and knead up the curls.
Leave the roots dark.
Lighten only the spots you can see.

You don't care for mistakes.
You don't care about mistakes.
I missed a spot. We'll go back over it.

There is fear
of the process or the aftermath
of moving too fast.

RSVP TO THE QUEER PROM
TIME TRAVEL PARTY

Our future selves dress us and send us off.

I grip seventeen-year-old me by the lapels of his ill-fitting suit, lift, and slip the jacket off his shoulders. Dress him in a kilt – tie-dye T-shirt that matches his Doc Marten boots, broken in. Roll his socks down for dancing. Look him in the eyes with a parting note of advice.

Our future selves watch from the bandstands.

The gymnasium fills with soon-to-be friends and soon-to-be-out friends. Each smiling cheek filled with a whole spectrum of light.

Our future selves reminisce their own crossed paths.

They grow from too chicken to ask to innocent dancing. The music is dire. Authentic adolescence. Watch them learn from each other, how they move in their bodies. Open up arms in each other's presence. Feed off the energy of experimentation. Meet eyes with a smile. Be close and feel safe.

Our future selves walk us home.

On this eve of leaving schools and suburbs, they catch a glimpse as themselves as they couldn't imagine. As they eventually will be.

I promise, you can build a life like tonight.

2040

We found a place to live together.
Two flats on the same landing.
Four bedrooms, two kitchens.
Two living rooms.
A study for me and you.

There's plants in every fireplace.
Candles on the mantle.
Forty years' worth of pictures
we're finally allowed to stick to the wall.
There's enough knowledge between us
to fix it up when we move on.

Two streets south lives Syd.
We've got him to commit
to Sunday dinners
and one holiday a year
with Owen and the kids
up at our bit.

There's a pizza place on the corner
for special occasions.

There's a pub with a pool table.
Neil's only gotten better.

There's a park in walking distance.
I can almost walk the dogs.

There's an open mic in a local café.
We try to make it home.

We have a garden front and back.
Okay, maybe it's not *ours*,

but we planted veg and herbs and flowers
and I'm still trying to grow some chillies.
The sun hits it five hours a day.
It's the time we call our break.

There's a place where this all happens.
There's a time where this makes sense.
There's a future where things work out,
where as a family we live.

ACKNOWLEDGEMENTS

Thank you: Bibi and Ellen, for many years of making me, and these poems, better.

Thank you: McFarlanes – a family I am so proud to have.

Thank you: Bridget, Clive and Harriet from Burning Eye for making this book with me.

Thank you: Fraser, Bibi, Dev, Neil and Syd for all the tattoos we share and those you have shared with me for this book's cover.

Thank you: to everyone who has opened up their lives and homes to me over the years – the world is shaking and even when we are not steady we are constant in our love.

Thank you for reading.